CU00902706

Contents

1934 - Preparing for the Air Race

KLM DC-2 - Passenger carrying for the Race

General view prior to the start

RAF MILDENHALL was opened in October 1934 as the first of the new style bomber bases as the Royal Air Force began its pre-war expansion but, before the first service unit arrived, was loaned to the Royal Aero Club for the start of the England to Australia GREAT AIR RACE.

The city of Melbourne was celebrating its centenary in 1934 and its Lord Mayor conceived the idea of an international air race as a means of focusing world attention on the city which had shared in the general economic depression of the 1930's.

Sir MacPherson Robertson, a millionaire sweet manufacturer whose career had been a classic story of rags to riches, agreed to sponsor the race but insisted that it be truly international and that everything possible be done to reduce the risk of accidents. He was mindful of the number of lives that had been lost in previous races to Australia such as that of 1919 when three of the five aircraft entered crashed with the loss of four lives; only one aircraft (a Vickers Vimy flown by Capt. Ross Smith) completed the course, taking 27 days 20 hours to do so. The record for the flight to Australia stood in 1934 at 8 days 20 hours 47 minutes, the holder being C. W. A. Scott who was to win this new race.

There was a dreadful suspicion that Britain was going to be humiliated in the race as there seemed to be no suitable British aircraft available but, in January 1934, the De Havilland Aircraft Company announced that it was building a new racing monoplane. This, the Comet, was designed and built in record time, three being purchased for entry in the race. A list of 63 competitors was published in July but numbers had reduced to 30 by the time the official programme was printed and eventually there were only 20 starters.

Here are some excerpts from the Competitors Handbook. They highlight the rudimentary nature of information at that time.

Note the avoidance of low flying around the Newmarket area due to racehorses.

INSTRUCTIONS FOR THE START

Reprinted from Supplementary Regulations III. MacRobertson International Air Races, issued by the Royal Aero Club.

1. **STARTING AERODROME.**—Mildenhall Aerodrome, Suffolk, has been selected as the starting point for the races. The aerodrome lies about 12 miles W.S.W. of Thetford, 18 miles N.E. of Cambridge and 9 miles N.N.E. of Newmarket.

2. **REPORTING.**—In accordance with Condition No. 16 (11) of the races the pilot in charge must report with his aircraft completely erected and bearing the necessary certificates of airworthiness at the starting point seven clear days before the commencement of the race or at such other time as is specified. The aerodrome will be open to competitors from Saturday, 13th October, 1934, and aircraft will be accepted up to 4.30 p.m. (16.30 hours G.M.T.) on Sunday, 14th October, 1934. **Any pilot not presenting himself and his aircraft as above by the time specified will render it liable to exclusion from the races.**

3. **TECHNICAL CHECKS.**—During the six days prior to the race each aircraft will be examined by the technical officials in order to obtain the necessary particulars for the handicappers and the official race log book. The checks will include an all up weighing test, with full tanks and load for the race, and any competitor whose all up weight with full tanks exceeds the maximum permissible load under his certificate of compliance with the I.C.A.N. requirements must be prepared to make such adjustments in the load as may be necessary. In all cases where tanks cannot be filled to capacity without exceeding the permitted load adequate means of checking the tank contents must be provided for calibration and sealing to obviate the necessity of having to drain and refill the tanks at control or other checking points.

4. **WEIGHING OF LARGE AIRCRAFT.**—The weighing of all aircraft up to a loaded weight of 10,000 lbs. will be undertaken at Mildenhall. Aircraft exceeding this laden weight will be required to proceed to Croydon or Martlesham for weighing and certification. To avoid delay it is suggested that competitors whose aircraft exceed this laden weight should communicate in advance with the Secretary of the Royal Aero Club in order that arrangements may be made for them to be weighed at Croydon immediately prior to reporting at Mildenhall.

5. **EMERGENCY RATIONS.**—In accordance with Condition 16 (4) every competing aircraft must carry sufficient food and water to maintain life for the pilot and each member of the crew for three days. The minimum amount of drinking water in this connection has been fixed at 1½ gallons per person. The amount of food will be left to the discretion of each competitor subject to the officials in charge being satisfied that it is reasonable. Emergency rations, if carried in suitable containers and submitted for weighing and sealing prior to the start, may be included as pay-load for the purpose of the handicap race. The other emergency equipment required by the conditions, namely, lifebelts and smoke signals, will not be included in the pay-load.

6. **HANGAR ACCOMMODATION.**—Hangar accommodation is available at Mildenhall for all except the largest types of aircraft entered for the race and will be allocated as far as possible in order of arrival. Competitors having a wing span exceeding 80 feet may be required to picket in the open and should notify the Secretary of the Royal Aero Club in advance whether picketing gear or engine covers will be required.

7. **TEST FLIGHTS.**—After reporting at Mildenhall, competing aircraft are required to remain at the starting point until the commencement of the race (Condition 16 (11)) and test or other flights may be carried out only with the consent of the controlling authorities. The aerodrome is not equipped for night flying.

8. **LOW FLYING.**—The aerodrome is in the vicinity of a number of racing stables, particularly in the neighbourhood of Newmarket. **All pilots, therefore, both on arrival and during any practice flights are requested to avoid all low flying particularly in the neighbourhood of Newmarket where serious damage might be occasioned to the racehorses.**

9. **STARTING TIMES AND PROCEDURE.**—The start will take place at 6.30 a.m. (06.30 hours G.M.T.) on Saturday, 20th October, or as soon thereafter as conditions of weather and visibility permit. Competitors will be despatched at short intervals, the necessary corrections in time being made at the Singapore control which will be notified by wireless of the exact starting time of each aircraft. Subject to unforeseen delays it is anticipated that the maximum period of adjustment at Singapore will not exceed 30 minutes. During the period of adjustment at Singapore, no work on the aircraft may be carried out, but the pilots and crew will be free to leave the machine and attend to any personal requirements such as meals, etc.

10. **COMPETITORS' MEETING.**—There will be a meeting of all competitors in the Competitors' Lounge Marquee at Mildenhall, at 5.30 p.m. (17.30 hours G.M.T.) on Sunday, 14th October, 1934, when the preliminary organisation will be explained in detail. **It is essential that the chief pilot of every competing aircraft (or an authorised person who will accept responsibility on behalf of such pilot) should be present at the meeting.**

Below are a couple of examples, again from the Competitors Handbook showing the level of information available for the control point airfields. These also show the facilities to be expected.

Darwin highlights the basics in that era with the telephone being available at the local Fanny Bay Gaol and minor repairs could be carried out at the Meat Works. The Gaol was illuminated by searchlight.

Allahabad had railway workshops available for repairs.

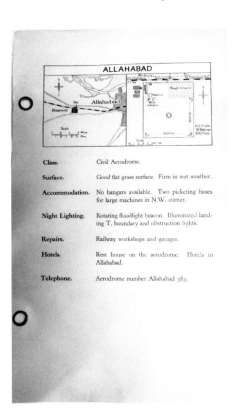

Class.	Civil Aerodrome.
Surface.	Good flat grass surface. Firm in wet weather.
Accommodation.	No hangars available. Two picketing bases for large machines in N.W. corner.
Night Lighting.	Rotating floodlight beacon. Illuminated landing T, boundary and obstruction lights.
Repairs.	Railway workshops and garages.
Hotels.	Rest house on the aerodrome. Hotels in Allahabad.
Telephone.	Aerodrome number Allahabad 383.

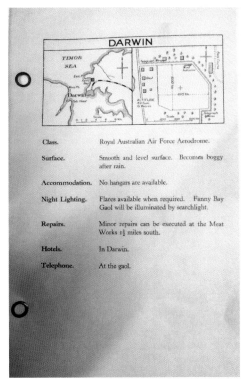

Class.	Royal Australian Air Force Aerodrome.
Surface.	Smooth and level surface. Becomes boggy after rain.
Accommodation.	No hangars are available.
Night Lighting.	Flares available when required. Fanny Bay Gaol will be illuminated by searchlight.
Repairs.	Minor repairs can be executed at the Meat Works 1½ miles south.
Hotels.	In Darwin.
Telephone.	At the gaol.

According to the Clerk of the Course's diary for this event, RAF Mildenhall was not the first choice to play host. That fell to Hatfield but as practical considerations were identified, it was realised that Hatfield would not be able to accommodate the expected number of entrants. As the net widened for something that would work, RAF Mildenhall showed promise. It was not yet operational, it had a considerable grass airfield and 2 large empty hangars. As an aside, Mildenhall being so far from London it was not expected to become a magnet for too many spectators. Famous last words.

Activity really started from Saturday 13ᵗʰ October with the arrival of the Officials. Facilities were rather sparse as the airfield was still very much under construction and so tenting arrangements were put in place. On the positive side, a telephone exchange was installed in one of the outbuildings. The problem was also compounded as it coincided with Newmarket horse racing so most accommodation in the area had already been taken. Aircraft started to arrive from later that day.

Most aircraft started to arrive on the Sunday and so did the spectators. Security became a more serious issue as the event progressed and the number of police was doubled from 6 to 12 on Friday, bearing in mind that numbers of spectators were already moving into the tens of thousands. Wednesday had seen a draughting of 80 cadets from RAF Cranwell to assist. Fencing incursions increased rapidly during the week as people wanted to view the arrivals. Some of which were more eventful than others. The Mollisson's Black Magic for example had to make 3 attempts at landing. The weather was recorded as chilly with a strong north westerly breeze that persisted for most of the week.

There were over 20 checks that needed to be completed on each aircraft ensuring they conformed to the requirements of the competition. These were time consuming both for the officials as the crew. For example, unfortunately the Irish entry failed to meet the weight limits and was forced to withdraw. Also one Fairey IIIF aircraft was classified such that the category it was in had a speed expectation more than 20mph faster than it was capable of. Many were sympathetic to the plight as any hope of attaining a respectable place were dashed before it flew. There were many more incidents of tweaking needed to comply with the regulations especially within weight limits. Not many aircraft had radio equipment but those that did were given special dispensation so that the crew could use it without a radio licence.

However the event had caught the public imagination and numbers kept increasing at Mildenhall to watch the preparations. As the pressure kept increasing news came that the Prince of Wales would be arriving by aeroplane followed in the afternoon by King George V who, with Queen Mary and the Prince of Wales, toured the airfield on that Friday, 19th October. This being the first of many royal visits to RAF Mildenhall over the years.

Estimates vary as to how many spectators had gathered for that 6:30 start on the Saturday but are in the region of 60,000 - 70,000. The traffic jams were the worst that had ever been seen in the district which was then only served by narrow country lanes. It was estimated that over 5000 spectators had surged onto the airfield just prior to takeoff. Luckily common sense prevailed and they backed off to form rows either side of the strip. The race was started at 6.30 a.m. by the Lord Mayor of London and the first to take off was the Comet flown by Amy Johnson and Jim Mollison, the others following at

45 second intervals. All 3 Comets struggled with the takeoff being at maximum weight. Others including the DC-2 made it look very calm and easy. The green Comet of Cathcart Jones & Waller had to abort the first attempt and while taxiing back there was a heart stopping moment when no 6 the Dutch Pander S4 begins its takeoff run at the returning Comet. With true professionalism of a long standing airmail pilot Geysendorfer alters the take off run sufficiently to avoid any incident. The green comet then had to wait for the next available slot in the 45 second schedule for a satisfactory takeoff. However in less than 17 minutes they were all airborne.

The progress of the race was headline news for days to come. The favourites, the Comets and the DC-2, kept ahead of all the others. The Mollisons reached Baghdad non-stop on the first day but had to withdraw on the 22nd October with engine trouble. Scott and Black raced on to arrive first at Melbourne in a record time of 70 hours 54 minutes 18 seconds. The flight on the leg to Singapore was hindered by violent storms and crossing the Timor Sea they suffered from an engine failure, not advisable when flying over shark infested waters.

The DC-2 arrived next, in 90 hours 13 minutes, to win the Handicap Race, an incredible performance for a commercial airliner. They had issues on the last leg across Australia which is an amazing story in it's own right. Reference Podcast in Suggested further Reading

Many still remember this as the greatest air race of all time. It was certainly a competition which proved the worth of many of the aircraft taking part. The Comet later developed into the Mosquito, the DC-2 into the DC-3 (known also as the Dakota or C-47) and, the Boeing led to the B-17 Flying Fortress.

1934 - Preparing for the Air Race

Pander S4 Postjager - Media attention

Stack & Turner - Airspeed A.S.8 Viceroy - Withdrew at Athens

1934 - Preparing for the Air Race

The Grass Runway being cleared

It was a time of improvisation as no
windsock had been erected

1934 - Preparing for the Air Race

Cuthcart-Jones & Waller - DH.88 - completed the Race

Jimmy Melrose - DH-80 - completed the Race

RAF Mildenhall - Now & Then

February 2024
Reference points
1 Hangar
2 Hangar
3 Middleton Hall

September 1934
Reference points
1 Hangar
2 Hangar
3 Middleton Hall

14

The dust has settled and euphoria has passed, spectators have left and life now returns to normal. As time also moves forward a few decades the desire to commemorate the anniversary arises. A shout out from Mildenhall Museum for memories of that event 65 years in the past results in the following transcripts which give a fascinating insight into the impact that it had locally.

MEMORIES OF THE AIR RACE

We set off early - about four o'clock and walked up Field Road to the airbase.

We walked in the ditch and in the fields as there was so much traffic. I remember the sun rising red in the sky. It was a beautiful morning. I wore a summery dress and straw hat - we all wore hats in those days. Just before we got to, what is now Spy Corner, a plane came down, out came Florence Desmond and Black (he was in the race). She came out onto the road, she was wearing a long dress and silver shoes and had a helmet on. (He wanted to marry her but went on the flight. She put a gold cigarette case in the cockpit - if he came back answer was in there!).

Saw Amy Johnson go off into the sunrise.

There was a Dutch plane which wouldn't go. They all threw their hats in the air when it started. We watched them all go.

There were thousands of people.

Amy Johnson stayed at the Bull.

[From notes made by Chris Mycock in conversation with Lily, 62 in 1990 who took her son Cecil aged 6 at the time of the Air Race.]

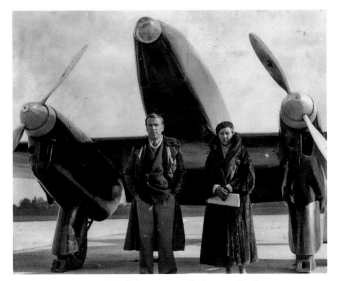

Jim Mollison and Amy Johnson

Start of the Race

MILDENHALL TUESDAY 16.10.34

Dear Con & Arthur

Just a few lines hoping you are both keeping well and not too busy, glad to say we are both nicely.

Now mate I wonder if you could manage to get a frame out for me as soon as possible, I want one 18" x 14" to take a black & white photo and not too expensive, i shall be glad if you can manage it for me sometime soon.

I expect you are disappointed you cannot get down here this week aren't you, well mate as I know you are so interested in planes I have decided to chance whether you will really be interested and give you my own version of what it is like living in Mildenhall since it has been put on the map, although I am afraid I am not exactly a press reporter and also I am sure you will realise that we do not get a lot of opportunity actually in the town here of seeing much of the planes but still I think you will be interested to know what little I can tell you, & it will give you rather a better idea than you can glean from the papers, so I will try and make it as interesting as possible starting from last Saturday when the actual fun began.

Saturday

From early morning there was a feeling of excitement everywhere as this was the day we were really going to be put on the map, and everyone was wondering what exactly was going to happen. Things soon began to move as by 8.30am huge petrol lorries were coming through and following these began a stream of cars containing officials of the Royal Aero Club, about midday a huge coach arrived full of Aero Club merchants.

This stream continued all through the afternoon but no signs of any planes however at about 5.15pm with a terrific roar one came over and banked steeply and went straight down, this was an American Machine (Baby Ruth) piloted by J H  Wright the type of machine being a Lambert Monocoupe and it has been estimated that at the time of touching the ground he was travelling at 95 M.P.H. it will give you a little idea of the noise when I say it was impossible to hear yourself speak as it went over. Later in the evening we learnt that another had arrived that one being a Dutch plane  (Desoutter Mark 11) piloted by Levit M Hansen.

Sunday

By 6 am cars were coming through in a continuous stream and by dinner time we heard 3 more racing planes had arrived 2 of them being Comets. At 1pm Pete arrived here from Icklingham and we both started straight away to spend the afternoon there, & I can tell you it was a sight I shall never forget, it was one continual stream of traffic the whole way in spite of the bitterly cold wind, on our arrival there we were just in time to see a plane coming in the distance and further out were two planes on petrol duty, this plane gradually came nearer & circled round and came down, quite near to where we were standing, as soon as

it landed mechanics were running out to it and two vans with Cinema Cameras fitted on top with a man operating them were soon busy, these belonged to British Gaumont Pictures and Movietones, it was gradually brought up to the Hanger nearest to us & out of it stepped C.J. Melrose the one that flew from Australia to England in 10 days, the machine was a D H Moth pale blue in colour.

A little later another one or two arrived but we did not get very good views of them when landed as they went into the other Hanger which we could not see very well. Gradually the time crept on until a lovely machine came roaring over cream in colour edged with red, this came down quite close to us, this time the pilot being Capt. T. Neville Stack with an Airspeed A.S.8.

By this time I had managed to get into conversation with a chap that had been there all day & he told me that the Mollisons (Amy & Jim) had not arrived so theirs was the third comet and we were hoping that we should be lucky enough to see them.

20

A few minutes later there was a roar behind us & over came another lovely machine & again it landed quite near to us, this proved to be an Airspeed Courier A.S.5 entered by Aircraft Exchange & Mart and piloted by Squadron Leader Stodart, and it certainly looked a very useful machine too.

The time gradually kept slipping away until about 2.45pm a tiny black spot could be seen, it did not look bigger than dot but in about 30 seconds with a terrific roar it was over us and with my field glasses I managed to get its number 63, I turned to my bloke with the programme standing by me and we hurriedly looked to find out who this was as it was very high up and you can imagine our feelings when we saw in the programme No 63 D.H. Comet, Pilots Mr and Mrs Mollison. So we were going to see them after all, again they circled round still too high to land & going at a terrific pace, again they came round lower and right over us, they came round and attempted to land but came up again right over us at about 50 feet and we had a glorious view of Jim piloting & Amy waving from the back seat. Another odd plane or two came about & just as we left an Imperial Airways came down with a load of passengers. We had to walk into West Row and it was an awful job all the way back for traffic -one estimate I have heard is 15,000 cars & 40-50,000 people.

Monday

Much quieter but about midday Capt. Stack was testing out and I heard he done well over 200 M.P.H. we saw it quite well, all quiet during the afternoon but about 5.15pm there was another terrific roar Jimmy Woods the Australian had arrived.

Tuesday

This morning about 10.30am another plane came over but although we saw it we could not say definitely who it was although one rumour I have heard is that it is Ronny the American that has been held up for delivery of his machine and that he had flown from America in 12.5 hours, but I rather doubt if this is correct.

At 3.30pm, as a matter of fact while I was writing yesterday's report there was another roar & I made it into the Market Place just in time to see another, which I believe is the machine entered by the Irish Hospitals Sweep.

Now I think this is about all for now, except that Amy & Jim were in Mildenhall yesterday morning.

Let me know if this has been interesting to you, if so I will try and let you have another epistle about the remaining part of the week up to the start

Cheerio for now

Love from us both

Yours as ever
Fre & Alf

[This letter was written by Alfred Grantham then living at 3 Market Place, Mildenhall with his brother in law

References to people mentioned:
Fre: Freda Grantham, my mother
Con: Elsie C Turner my mother's sister
Pete: My maternal grandfather David Wright of Icklingham
Dad: My paternal grand father Alfred Grantham Snr of Barton Mills]

MILDENHALL Tuesday 23.10.34

Just a few lines hoping you are both well also to thank you for getting the frame through so quickly for me, sorry that I did not have time to enclose a letter with prints yesterday.

Glad to say we are both keeping nicely, Fre has gone to Bury this afternoon. I was pleased to hear you were interested in my epistle of last Tuesday & as I promised to let you have another I will see what i can do now that all the excitement is over, but really I don't know if I shall manage to give you a very good idea of the scenes which took place here as it was one after the other so quickly that everyone seemed dazed, but those of us who were lucky enough to be here will remember last week until our dying day.

In my last letter I gave you the news up to Tuesday, now I will try & give you our experiences from then.

<u>Wednesday</u> nothing very startling happened, just a few trial flights.

<u>Thursday</u> morning numerous people making for aerodrome.

<u>Thursday</u> afternoon Gordon King and myself went to

aerodrome, just arrived in time to see Amy Mollison take "Black Magic" up by herself for the first time, we were very curious to see what sort of a hand she would make of it as Jim was hopeless at landing, however she made a perfect take off and also very good landing so that looked a little more hopeful for one of Britain's hopes.

Soon after this we decided to sport 5 bob on the drome and have a good look all round the machines both in the hangars and outside as well, so on we went & found there were guides told off to take people round & explain everything so we were well away, my word it was an education in itself & we did enjoy it, here are one or two items that may interest you.

1. The Dutch Air Liner when loaded has 3 tons of petrol on board

2. The American Plane piloted by Rosco Turner is fitted with a wireless set capable of picking up every station in the world.

3. The Comets cannot get into top gear until 1000 feet up.

4. Melrose the 21 year old Australian has a job to squeeze into his seat it is so narrow and he has petrol tanks to lean his back against.

After we had seen all that was to be seen in the hangars we strolled round outside watching the various planes being brought out and tested etc.

We both had copies of "The Aeroplane" with us, a paper that has been in great demand down here which gives pictures of the planes & their pilots so we thought it would be great if

we could get these autographed so decided to try & hunt up a few of the pilots in the hope of getting their signatures. We soon dropped across Capt Jack Wright pilot of "Baby Ruth" & tried him & we were very bucked when he said "Yes certainly" after that we got Davies, Waller & Melrose so you will bet we were pleased. I am sure you will be interested to see this souvenir.

Later we saw the Green Comet have her crash, as soon as she hit the ground a fire engine & 2 ambulances were dashing across to her, but luckily no one was hurt. just as I was leaving "Baby Ruth" went up & and it was the finest exhibition of aerobatics I have ever seen, for one thing he was looping the loop & rolling over sideways at over 100 miles per hour.

Thus ended my experiences for that day, an afternoon I shall ever remember but one that made me realise what a terribly dangerous task they were undertaking & the frailness of the machines holding these huge engines.

<u>Friday</u> From fairly early in the morning there was a steady stream of traffic for this was the day the Prince of Wales was inspecting the machines & later it became known the King & Queen were also coming of course the traffic got thicker.

I did not see anything of them as it was a pretty busy day in the shop & you would have laughed if you could have seen me about 8.30pm as I had 2 Dutchmen in for Cigarettes and neither of them could speak English, I think that was about the funniest experience lever had as we were all trying to make one another understand at the same time.

Friday night
10pm Several cars keep going through.
11pm Cars getting thicker.
12pm Impossible to sleep, cars roaring through without a break.

Saturday
5 AM Got up & opened shop after a sleepless night, & the sight which met my eyes I shall never forget as the main street was lined with cars & cycles 4 abreast & hardly moving so densely were they packed.

So this was the great morning, & the Wireless forecast of the previous night saying 20,000 people were expected has been smashed over & over again.

5.30 AM Dad arrived from Barton Mills as we were going to see the start from the Church Steeple he said he had never seen such a sight as by this time the traffic seemed thicker than ever if possible.

6 AM We make our way for the Church, it took us 10 minutes to cross the road & eventually got to the top of the Tower. The sight that met our eyes then is past all description, as no matter which way you looked the roads were packed as far as the eye could see & as they were all lit up it made it all the more impressive.

<u>6.15 AM</u> The dawn was gradually breaking, a lovely red glow was coming up from the east & it looked like being a perfect morning for the great send off, car lights were extinguished but the traffic was still as thick as ever.

<u>6.20 AM</u> Crowds dumping their cars on the road sides & over on foot across the fields in all directions, realising that it is there only chance of getting a glimpse of the planes.

<u>6.25 AM</u> Gradually the seconds keep slipping by and there is a death like silence as the roar of an engine starting up is heard by all.

<u>6.30 AM</u> as the clock ticks to the half hour how the silence is awful, not the roar of cheering one might expect instead the crowd stand breathless, while many a head turns skyward whilst a silent prayer is asked for the safety of these men & women who are about to fly to - who knows. As the clock strikes a deafening roar is heard & the first plane (Mollison's) can be seen roaring across the drome & gradually see rises, quickly to be followed by a second, a third & so on.

In less time than it takes to write this they are roaring over us heading straight into the glow of the rising sun with many a heartfelt wish going with them, and leaving behind them a feeling of great sadness.

All is complete silence until the last is completely out of sight & then all is bustle & commotion once again & the homeward trek has commenced. So ends a week every inhabitant of Mildenhall will remember until their dying day.

I really shall have to pack this job soon or you will be properly fed up with me, but these are just a few items that I have learnt since Saturday which will probably interest you, & all of these I can personally vouch for as they are quite correct & not just rumours.

All the car parks in Beck Row were full by midnight Friday one man with a small field some distance from the Drome charged 1/- for every car parked there Saturday morning & he took £45.

There were people from as far away as Glasgow, Edinburgh, Holland, France & Germany.

In Kenny Hill which as you know is miles from anywhere there were 5,573 cars in 2 hours.

There were cyclists from London & places quite as far if no further.

Hagger was open all night and was packed out the whole time.

Of course it is impossible to say how many people were but there is no doubt the papers are hopelessly out of it when they say 60,000, personally taking the census of Kenny Hill & one I heard on the outskirts of Mildenhall I should not think 50,000 cars and 200,000 people is over estimating it.

Now mate I really must close, hoping you will not too fed up with this lot.
Hoping to see you again soon
Yours as ever Fre & Alf

PS. Great excitement today when Mildenhall heard the great news of Scott, once again England has shown the way.

Wed 13 Aug
My dear Stephanie

I am afraid I haven't much news for you regarding The Air Race. I can only remember my Mother's house was full of Reporters. The town was packed! We walked all the way to the Drome mostly in the Dark because street lighting was all by gas & not much of it! because there weren't many houses past the Mildenhall School.

Goodys Husband (Charlie) used to work at the old Gasworks by the mill & he had to go all round the Town lighting the lights & putting them out again in the morning.

We had to walk all the way on the grass verges as the Road was packed. Although we did see Amy Johnson & Jim Mollison etc they were muffled up & as I said it was pitch dark. I think I was about 21 at the time. I am now 96 so would it have been about that time?

Mike took us to Old Warden some time ago. Air displays of course!

Men were working on the original Comet - a year or two later they had finished restoring it & it was flying again. Mike took us over to the Commentator when the show was over & after chatting about the Plane. Mike told him I had actually seen it take off all those years ago. He was quite stunned!!!

I'm afraid I have been rambling on for a long time without giving you much information but I'm afraid that's all I know.

Please forgive the lined paper I'm all over the place if I write on plain sorry about scribble on back of page get short of paper now.

Hoping you are all keeping well so pleased to say we are all fine here.

In reply to your letter concerning the Air Race of 1934.

I was nine years old at the time and staying with my grandparents Mr and Mrs Walter Clarke at 11, Market Place. I was thrilled to know that Amy Johnson would be staying the night before the race at their house.

I remember well seeing her arrival as I stood in the hallway, a smallish person among several men.

It was exciting the next morning when in the early hours and still dark, my grandfather took me to the airfield.

Standing back in the crowd I was amazed at all the different planes and their different colours. One stands out  particularly in my mind as it was larger than the rest and coloured a pretty pale greeny blue. I think it was a Dutch plane. I was very interested in all the very smartly dressed ladies in their lovely clothes mingling with the men around the planes.

We watched them all take off and my grandfather bought me a big wall map from the souvenir sellers going round the watching crowd. I took it when I went back to school in Newmarket and it was put on the wall and we marked the progress of the various planes on the route and their places in the race.

These are my memories and hopefully they may of some small help.
Yours sincerely
B.M. KROJEIWSKA (Mrs)

THE FIRST MILDENHALL - MELBOURNE AIR RACE

I went to Mildenhall Aerodrome the afternoon before the Race started to see the aeroplanes. The public could not get very near to them, but I always was a lucky chap, and as I was looking through the gate a traveller friend of mine came along and said: "Hello Mr. Lawson, come in with me I have a pass". He was the Representative for Lodge Plugs.

He took me round all the 'planes and we saw all the Pilots getting ready and chatted to some, including Mr. Mollison and Amy Johnson.

They were just going up to test the Comet and he let Amy take the pilot's seat. They had a spin round and, when they landed, Amy let it bump down too steep and it tipped upon its nose and smashed the propeller.

They both came back to where we were and they had the devil of a row, right in front of us and lots of other people. My word, he did swear at her.

They had to get a new propeller flown over from France. It arrived in time and was fitted that night.

When I told my Garage Foreman, Bill Lankester, he said: Lets go over early in the morning and see them start, and why don't we each ask our landladies to come? It will be a treat for them, and they will then have to get up & cook breakfast for us! (Clever boy!). This was a really good thought. They were delighted, and were very grateful.

We got to Mildenhall early but only just in time; the cars were already pulling up on the edge of the road with their bumper bars against the Aerodrome chain link fence. We got a lovely spot where we could see all the 'planes start, and the one on the perimeter right close to us was the

oldest one in the race. We saw the two men get in and take off. They never got there - they were both killed.

If we had not been early we would never have got near. Cars arrived in their hundreds and every road for miles around was jammed full. They drove their cars on to the grass verge or into fields and got out and walked.

The Gentleman who drove up to the Aerodrome fence just in front of me and was immediately on my right was a fairly large fat man with a Trilby hat. We had an hour or more to wait before the start, he was the only one in his car and he appeared to settle down to a doze.
When it was all over & people began to start up their engines and make a noise, he wound down his window and said to me "how long before they start?" I said "It's all over they are all gone. "Damn it he said I must have gone to sleep. I have come all the way from Scotland to see them start".
I hope he enjoyed his nap.

[By Cyril Lawson From Lawson's Coll. BSEems 1999-23]

J ust as I was coming up for my ninth birthday in 1934 I remember to this day being brutally woken up by my father in the early hours of a morning. "come on, get ready, we are going somewhere interesting" I got dressed quickly and went down the road to a neighbours house and my father tossed some pebbles up against an upstairs window to wake up his friend, Alf Brown, who appeared at the window in his pyjamas and gave a wave. Soon he came out of his front door fully dressed, unlocked his garage and backed out his little Austin Seven saloon. We got in and off we went, me still not knowing where we were going. In those days cars were still quite rare. There was only one other person in the whole of our housing estate owning one and so it came as a complete surprise at the top of our road to find lines of cars as far as  the eye could see. They were all evidently heading for the same place. Alf nosed his little car in to the first available gap and we were on our way. We are going to see some aeroplanes daddy said. It was a memorable journey and the first time in my life I saw a streamlined vehicle, and of all the hundreds, it was the only one like it. Arriving at our destination, Mildenhall, my first recollection is of a long row of assorted aeroplanes with one enormous biplane as the centrepiece. The masses of people were allowed to wander fairly close to have a look, but were then shooed away and made to stand back ready for the start of the first really great air race which was to Australia. Great cheers went up as each plane took off and headed away into the distance. I don't remember the great names of all the pioneer pilots, but I particularly remember Scott and Black who went on to win the race. At the time very few people even had wirelesses. But my father had brought home a collection of bits and pieces which he wired together including an accumulator and a loudspeaker spread all over the kitchen table and he got it to crackle and we could hear voices from the speaker but not good enough for us to understand when they were saying about the air race. We had to wait for the newspaper to be able to find out more.

I am grateful that my father and Alf Brown took me to witness such a spectacular event. Alf Brown went on in partnership with Paddy Harris to start the very first efficient taxi service in Cambridge. The firm was called Camtax and was equipped with Ford Luxicabs. Astonishing vehicles way ahead of the times.

The Great Air Race of 1934 As a 9 year old Don MacKay of Cambridge was taken by his father to watch take off

I was There

Between six and seven o'clock on the morning of Saturday, 20 October, 1934, a number of aircraft took off, one by one, in the biggest air race of all time. This was the MacRobertson International Air Race - named after Sir MacPherson Robertson, a wealthy Australian. The race was programmed as being from London to Melbourne.

The point of departure was the airfield at Mildenhall, in Suffolk, seventy miles north of London and close to the borders of Cambridgeshire and Norfolk. The original airfield was located in and between the villages of Beck Row and West Row. Both of these were a mile or so from Mildenhall, which missed the main road from London to Norwich by a similar margin. Some nine miles from Newmarket and twelve from Bury St. Edmunds, Mildenhall was a small quiet, sleepy little town where nothing significant ever seemed to happen. Even so reference to it in a little poem in one of the London newspapers ending with the words: "they chose that dust-heap, Mildenhall" was rather unkind.

Mildenhall had seen a lot of history long before the advent of flying machines, figuring prominently in the time of Hereward the Wake and his defiance of the Norman conquerors. For hundreds of years its fine old church had watched over the picturesque market cross where weekly markets were maintained even when business declined.

On the day of the race an estimated sixty-thousand people

came to see it begin and little old Mildenhall had never seen anything quite like it. Perhaps my most vivid memory of that eventful day is standing at the window of my parents' bedroom. My father and mother were still in bed, because at half-past five in the morning it was still dark. In those days only a small proportion of people owned cars, but looking from the window I could see a never-ending procession of headlights and I could feel the urgency of the drivers as they moved slowly along, bumper to bumper.

Such was the volume of traffic that many of the cars did not reach the airfield in time. I don't remember seeing any signs and not being familiar with the locality most of the drivers could only make a wild guess as to how much further the airfield was. Consequently cars were parked erratically with some of them even encroaching on to the carriageway.

For a fifteen-year-old boy this was real excitement. I would not have believed that there were so many cars in the whole world. Nothing like this had ever happened before and my enthusiasm knew no bounds. Mostly cars were either crawling or stopped completely and in these circumstances I had something better than a car, I had a bicycle. It was no trouble to weave my way between and around obstructions and still maintain a reasonable speed. More by luck than good management I arrived in time to see most of the aircraft take off, although I may have missed a couple. Regrettably, at that stage I did not know one plane from another, but it was very thrilling and stimulating.

One of the visitors was a real opportunist. He threw open the gate of a large field and then took parking fees off motorists until it was full to capacity. Then he quietly disappeared.

The winner of the race which I followed with interest, was a De Haviland Comet piloted by C.W.A. Scott and T Campbell Black. Another Comet, piloted by Amy Johnson and Jim Mollison, started off well but (as I remember) was the victim of fuel mismanagement.

There is no doubt that this race was a unique event in aviation history. Because of it, the flying time from Europe to the Far East was halved and the way paved for long distance commercial aviation. It led to the development of a revolutionary British aircraft, the De Haviland Comet and it also demonstrated the power and skill of American engineering, with special reference to the great aircraft companies, Douglas and Boeing.

Another milestone was the bringing together of many renowned pilots of the heroic, pioneer age of aviation. These included Scott and Campbell Black, Amy Johnson and Jim Mollison, Roscoe Turner, Parer, Stack, Parmentier and Melrose (from Adelaide). Modern aviation, as far as Australia was concerned, was born in 1934.

This event made a profound impression on my young mind. The very idea of flying all the way to Australia captured my imagination. After Neville Chamberlain went to see Hitler in September, 1938, big advertisements began to appear in the daily newspapers using young men to join the services. War was coming - that was a foregone conclusion - and here was an opportunity to do two things, to work on aeroplanes and be in it from the start. Consequently, in November, 1938, against all the rules of common sense (I was just coming to the end of my apprenticeship) I joined the Royal Air Force for six years as a Flight Rigger.

That decision may well have saved my life, but I was not to know that most Mildenhall boys of my age group would be captured by the Japanese in Singapore. Many of them did not come back.

[Rupert Charles Morley]

Local History Collection Margery Frape

[Unpublished Article by Charles Morley reproduced by kind permission of Mrs. Phyllis Morley]

Mildenhall Airfield

The initial airfield was built on land in the village Row, a part of West Row, I think that my father said it was 300 acres, and the actual airfield was laid down to grass grazed by sheep and parts cut for hay.

I was born in a cottage on the edge of the aerodrome nearly opposite the old "Bird in Hand" Public House, and within earshot of "Benny the Blacksmith's" at work on his anvil. Before the airfield was built, I used to go bird nesting with my brother john, cousin Gerald Fincham and a man called Fella Moss (who smoked a bulls head pipe) in the hedges of arable fields (the best land in Beck Row).

I remember steam engines coming and pulling the trees and hedges out, my father who farmed nearby helped to clear and burn the hedges and roots, this would be about 1932. He also helped to build the aerodrome with his horses and carts, moving bricks, sand and cement (bags) as Newport steam wagons had to unload before leaving firm ground. This work on building provided much employment for men from the town of Mildenhall and village of Lakenheath who on their way home on their 'bikes, we boys used to snow ball them in snowy weather. My father with his horses carted all the earth away for the first hangers foundations which were built, the dragline excavators dumping ½ of a ton a time into the tumbrels (carts) which was a load for the faithful horses. (Wonder what they would have thought to the huge American ones shown in your 'photos!).

After a while a little canteen was started and a man used

to come round with a little tray of goodies containing amongst other things mars bars. I think that this is when they first came out. My father used to purchase one of these mars bars and cut it in half with his shut knife. He would eat half of it and bring the rest home and say whose turn is it today!

I remember plainly the Mildenhall - Melbourne air race which took place in late October 1934, when the village of Beck Row became like London overnight, thousands of people came. It was estimated that about 70,000 (seventy thousand) spectators and 15,000 cars descended on this once quite village, besides bikes and cycles.

My father hired a meadow out for NCP (car parking) and my brothers and I cashed in well with bicycle parking fees.

The National Car Park man lodged with us and was kept busy all through the night and early morning as cars and motorbikes came just about all night and the race started off at 6.30 on the 20" October 1934. He used to come in to empty his leather strap bag over the table. He gave John and I tickets, three with the same number to use for bikes, one for the owner and one to stick on the mudguard and one to keep. We made good use of them at two or three pence each. Brother Arthur opened the gate to the aerodrome for Amy Johnson, who was world famous at this time and one of the contestants for the prize of £10,000 and a £500 gold cup (a lot of money in those days!)

I think that my sister Gwynneth's black cat "Janet" at the

same crossed the lane and she said "maybe good luck". It was a good job it was a clear morning, as misty fog would have delayed them at that time of year. Many other contestants from all countries with aeroplanes of various colours taking part could be seen flying around before the race began.

A tramp was doing well for a time on a piece of common land, towards Kenny Hill, taking fees for car parking until P C Hazel put a stop to him, occupants of cars thought he was a poor farmer!

The Garwoods (well known in Bury St Edmunds cattle market) had a mobile tea and refreshment stall on our lawn and did a good trade. It was early on a Saturday morning when the race began and they in turn started off.

Some of the locals were honoured in serving to pull the chock blocks away from the front of the 'plane wheels which were fixed to a chord, at a given signal. Many very colourful 'planes took part for this very long journey. There was a man among the vast crowd with a Gospel Text 'sandwich" board.

Our 'head' schoolmaster Mr P A Oldman of Beck Row C C School brought his wireless in the main room for us to hear the winning result, which I think was a man named Scott? On another occasion I can remember seeing a meadow full of tents, which I think were occupied by WRAF Girls stationed there for a short while. It may have been when H M King George V visited with the two princes - Edward and George. This must have been when my late cousin Hugh Bacon of West Row was pleased to record seeing three Kings in a Royal Chauffeur driven car, these were George V and his two sons, Edward and George

who later acceded to the throne of England. Photo taken 1935 My late cousin Fred Bacon (Hugh's brother) was a pilot officer who flew bomber planes in thirty raids over Germany without a scratch. He saw lots of his other squadron pals shot down and perish. He called to see my spinster aunts Edie and Nellie Bacon and slipped over on the doorstep and broke his arm! Later he went to South Africa to train pilots. I believe he may have been stationed at Beck Row Mildenhall for some of the time. After the war he became a Baptist minister warning his hearers of the brevity of life.

I remember sheep belonging to my Uncle Ed. Fincham, who lived opposite us, in the Sycamores, grazing the airfield and had a shepherd - Mr Alderton whose boys came to our school. My brother John and I sometimes helped with the sheep and watched them being "dipped", the local policeman in attendance. Cousin Gerald later on kept the sheep, and one morning was surprised to see a notice on the fold "Geraldo and his orchestra"!

I am in my mid 80's now, but can remember these events plainly and before the coming of the aerodrome we whipped our tops to school, void of traffic! Only I wish that some of those 'planes that went in the race, could have gone to the aid of 'Emperor Hallie Selassie of Ethiopia, whose land, at the same time, was being invaded in a brutal way by fascist dictator Benito Mussolini of Italy whose son Bruno piloted a 'plane and took part in air attacks on a defenceless people with poison mustard gas and recorded their ill gotten gains in the book "Wings over Ethiopia".

I can also remember the electricity coming to the aerodrome and the village. It was one very hot summer a gang of hard working Irishmen dug a trench beside the main road from Mildenhall to the aerodrome for the cable. They lodged in a tent on the triangular green in front of our cottage and came for water, which was drawn from a well at the back of the house. My mother had a busy time Saturday afternoons and Sundays, she would have to listen very carefully. I remember, when everything was quiet at night, seeing the watch-men's hut with his lamp and the lamps alongside the side of the deep trench. There he sat throughout the long night guarding.

These are my memories of the early days of Mildenhall Aerodrome in Beck Row. I think, that I am the only one left who actually lived more or less on this aerodrome and saw all that I have recorded here.

Yours sincerely

David V W Strawson

Gwynneth Elizabeth Strawson

Born 15th March 1927 at Beck Row

On 20th October 1934 I was 7 years and 7 months. I was born and lived at The Green, Beck Row. The road to Kenny Hill, Shippea Hill, West Row and Mildenhall ran past my house. In the 1930'S my father James Sallis Strawson and eldest brother Arthur were working with the horses preparing the land ready for the aerodrome.

My parents' back garden joined this land and by 1934 the runways and aerodrome buildings were completed.

(On the day of the air race) my father invited well known caterers, Mr and Mrs Garwood of Bury St Edmunds to park on the front lawn to serve teas. He also let out car parking space. He gave 2/6d to my older sister.

I had a black cat named Janet. I treated her like a doll and she was my best friend. The 20th October arrived after much hard work and excitement by all; it seemed that nobody had much sleep the previous night. I was watching the cars full of people arrive and my cat Janet was in my arms. The one drive way onto the aerodrome was by our side gate and I saw a very tall lady walking along, it was Amy Johnson. She spoke to me and stroked Janet and said that she hoped she would bring her luck. Sadly they had the wrong mix of fuel in the plane and Amy had to retire.

By E. Debenham, Lawshall, Bury St Edmunds.

Beryl Williams

My Memories of The 1934 Air Race
from MILDENHALL to AUSTRALIA

Great excitement for sometime before the race. The only pilots we had heard of were Amy and Jim Mollison so of course we wanted them to win.

At five o'clock on the morning of the great day I was woken up and taken to sit on a wall in North Terrace which was surrounding what was then called Gittas's field. It was subsequently hired by my father for farming purposes.

It seemed a long while that we waited but eventually the planes took off in the half light. It was soon over and I wondered why I was taken there but I was told it was a part of history which I would always remember.

The next day was exciting for us as we watched the London Taxis full of Ladies and Gentlemen driving past our house in Holywell Row Road (near Field Road) on their way back to London. They were mostly in evening dress which we admired very much. We would wave to these people and they would wave back. Mildenhall was as they say "On The Map".

Beryl Williams Mildenhall

47

S/Ldr. M. McGregor & H.C. Walker - Miles M.2F Hawk Major - 7d 16h

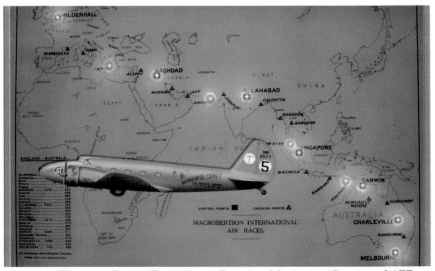

Roscoe Turner, Clyde Pangbom, Reeder Nichols - Boeing 247D - 92h 55min

The Crew, Aircraft & Achievement

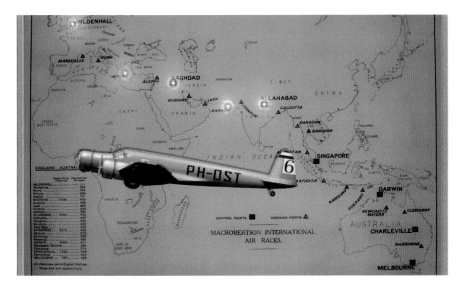

Gerrit Johannes, Geysendorfer, D.L. Asjes, P. Pronk -
Pander S4 Postjager - Destroyed Allahabad

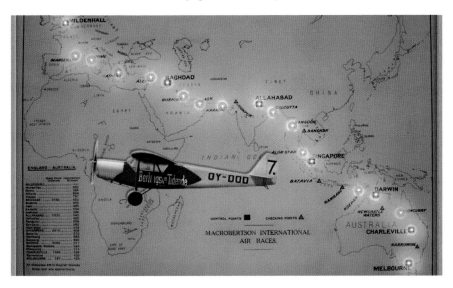

Lt. M Hansen, D Jensen - Desoutter Mark II - 31st October

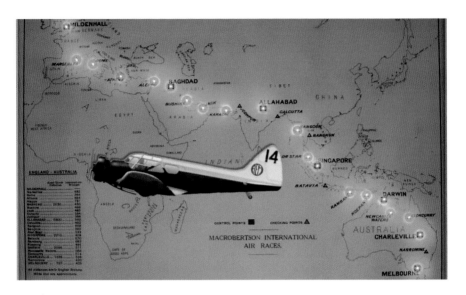

S/Ldr. D. Stodart, Sgt. Pilot K. Stodart - Airspeed AS.5 Courier -
9d 18h

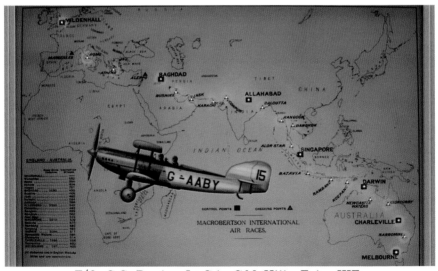

F/O. C.G. Davies, Lt.Cdr. C.N. Hill - Fairy IIIF -
Arrived 24th November

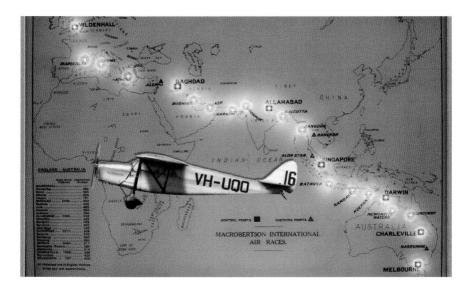

.J. Jimmy Melrose - DH.80 Puss Moth -
10d 16h

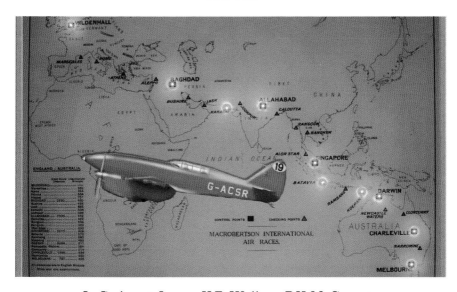

O. Cathcart Jones, K.F. Waller - DH.88 Comet -
108h 13min

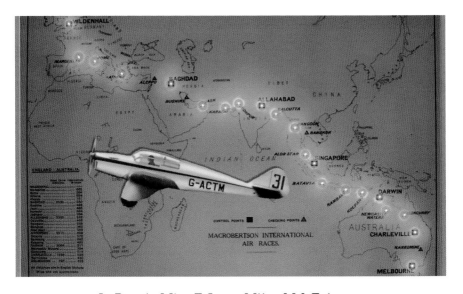

.L. Brook, Miss E Lay - Miles M.3 Falcon -
Arrived 20th November

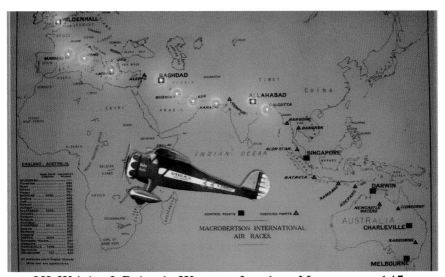

J.H. Wright, J. Polando Warner - Lambert Monocoupe 145 -
Withdrew at Calcutta

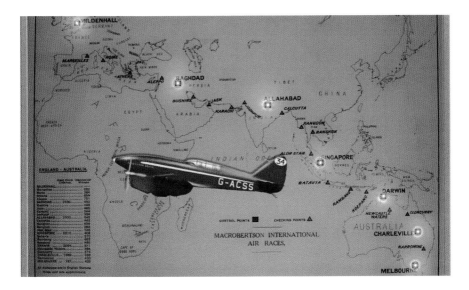

C.W.A. Scott, Tom Campbell Black - DH.88 Comet -
71h 0min

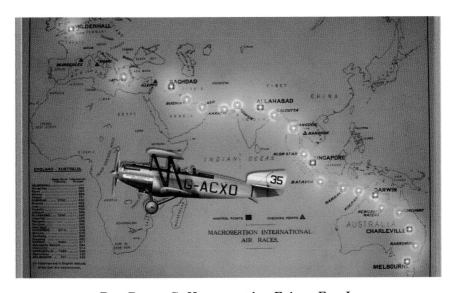

Ray Parer, G. Hemsworth - Fairey Fox I -
Arrived 13 February 1935

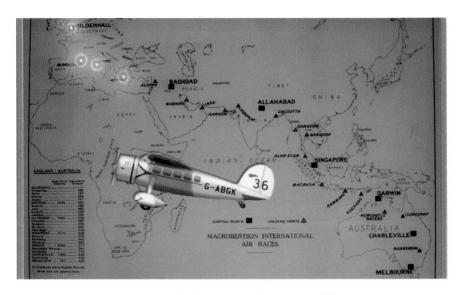

J. Woods, D.C. Bennet - Lockheed Vega -
Overturned at Aleppo

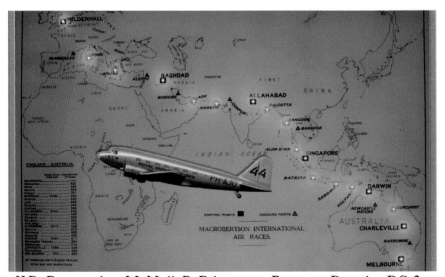

K.D. Parmentier, J.J. Moll, B. Prins, van Brugge - Douglas DC-2 -
90h 13mins

The Crew, Aircraft & Achievement

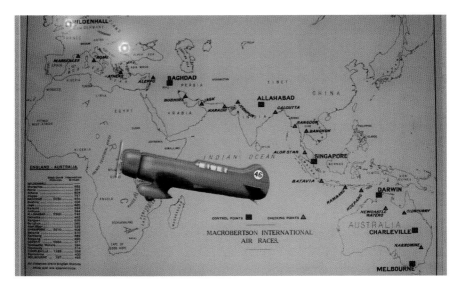

Jacqueline Cochran, W. Smith Pratt - Granville Gee Bee R-6H -
Withdrew at Bucharest

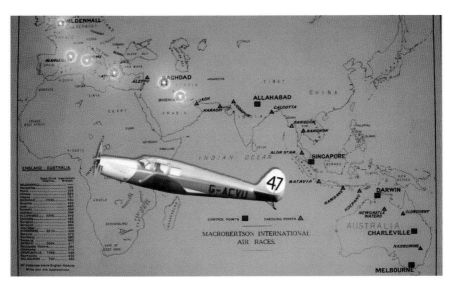

F/Lt G Shaw - B.A. Eagle -
Withdrew at Bushire

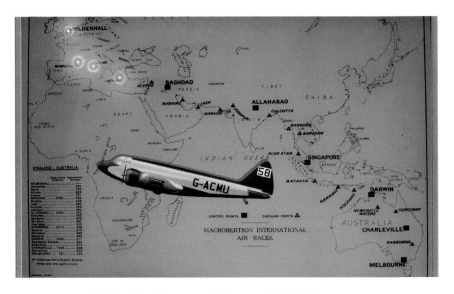

T. Neville Stack, - Airspeed AS.8 Viceroy -
Withdrew at Athens

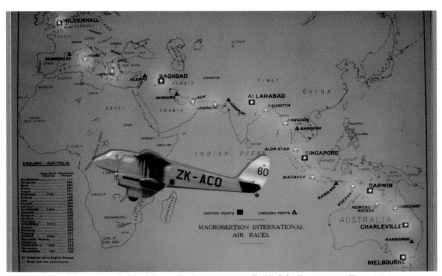

J.D. Hewitt, C.E. Kay, F. Stewart - DH.89 Dragon Rapide -
Arrived 3rd November

The Crew, Aircraft & Achievement

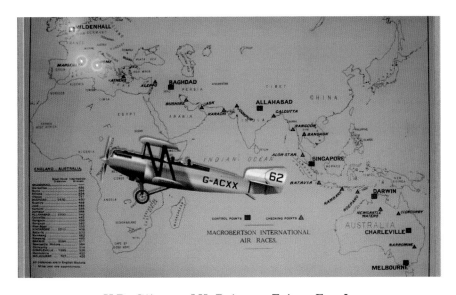

H.D. Gilman, J.K. Baines - Fairey Fox I -
Crashed nr Palazzo San Gervasio - No survivors

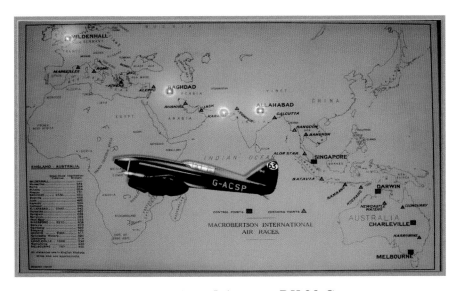

Jim Mollison, Amy Johnson - DH.88 Comet -
Withdrew at Jubulpur

Ithought it might be advantageous to add some footnotes to the achievements surrounding this race. In the era when most aircraft were still biplanes with open cockpits, we start to see the glimmers of future air transport. While all metal designs appear from the U.S.A. (DC-2 and Boeing 247) showing a future for passenger travel, the British provided an evolving view still based around the concept of a wooden structure (DH88 Comet).

The impetus behind this race did eventually create a catalyst showing the world that air travel really exists. We start to see more standard features like retractable undercarriage, variable pitch propellers, enclosed cockpits and radios. The concept of scheduled flights to far flung places now appeared to be realistic.

Focusing on the DH88 Comet as an example of what the race spurred designers to create, we see it took only 9 months from design start to first flight and that was only 6 weeks before the race. The Air Worthiness certificate was somewhat bland in recorded flight characteristics but permission was granted.

This aircraft was designed for really one purpose, to show the world that it was possible to design an aircraft for the race and to WIN. It was a balancing act between speed, weight and range in the design. This did evolve into the DH-98 Mosquito that excelled during WWII but had limited other potential.

The Comet did have retractable undercarriage, albeit by using what looked like a "steering wheel" attached to the starboard side of the cockpit. Turning it 14 times was used to both raise and lower the main wheels.

It also had variable pitch propellers, well 2 pitch settings (coarse and fine), whilst on the ground a bicycle pump was used to set the blades suitable for takeoff. As the airflow increased it forced a diaphragm to alter the pitch suitable for normal flight. Needless to say, not very practical in a hurry.

Radios were also on the "to do" list and not fitted neither was a full instrument panel for the rear (tandem) seat. Again a balance between weight and range. It was imperative for the aircraft to have the range so the priority was for carrying the fuel. Hence critical stages of the flight would either be carried out from the front seat or looking over the pilot's shoulder.

The crew would have less than 6 weeks to familiarise themselves with the aircraft before the race. As an example G-ACSS Grosvenor House (Scott and Campbell-Black) amassed 6 flights totalling approximately 2 hours before embarking on the epic flight.

The engines, Gipsy Six R variants were finely tuned and needed in-flight tweaking of the mixture for optimum performance. In fact all 3 crews - G-ACSP Black Magic (Jim and Amy Mollison), G-ACSR (Cathcart-Jones and Waller) - and G-ACSS Grosvenor House (Scott and Campbell-Black) all had significant problems maintaining a suitable equilibrium. The Mollisons did also fall foul of an incorrect low grade fuel at Jabalpur that put an end to their race.

These Comets were extremely fast for that era with the Mollisons establishing a new record by reaching Karachi in just over 22 hours. As both Mrs Lily Collen and Alf & Fre Grantham recalled, Black Magic led the pack into the skies at Mildenhall and were maintaining an excellent time until technical problems from Karachi onward. As mentioned they were then forced to retire at Jubulpur after having anything but an uneventful flight.

G-ACSS Grosvenor House on the other hand appeared to be "in the groove" amassing quite a lead over 2nd place DC-2 "Uiver. That was until halfway across the Timor Sea when oil pressure failed in the port engine. They limped into Darwin but the mechanics could not diagnose the problem. Scott and Campbell-Black were then forced to fly the remaining legs to Melbourne on one engine with the DC-2 just a few hours behind. Both pilots were needed to battle with the controls to keep the aircraft flying straight. It is said that Campbell-Black had to be helped out the cockpit due to his legs "locked" on the rudder pedals compensating the adverse yaw.

Turning attention to the KLM DC-2 "Uiver" aircraft, their entry proposed a different scenario. "Let's enter the race and take passengers as well". A forward thinking view if ever there was one and a very professional stance throughout.
Most of the flight turned out to be as expected - uneventful.

It was only really on the last leg that the weather decided to throw a wobbly. A night time flight from Charleville to Melbourne in adverse weather including electrical thunderstorms conspired to confuse the compass etc. They did however have a radio but too much static didn't help. Circumstances saw mountainous conditions with icing. The townsfolk could hear an aircraft droning around and realised a serious problem was ensuing. Using ingenuity and quick thinking, the Municipal Electrical Engineer turned the whole town Albury lights off and on, sending out Morse code to the aircraft. An abridged version of events saw cars turning up at the Albury race course with their lights on to highlight a landing zone. From being aware of an aircraft in difficulties to it landing it had only been about 20mins in the middle of the night. Taking off afterwards also needed the assistance of locals as the wheels settled in the soft ground. Some of the passengers and mail also had to be decamped to save weight for takeoff.

The podcast referred to at the end of the book elaborates more on events from the Australian perspective.

Close behind KLM's entry was the Boeing 247D leased by 'Colonel' Rosco Turner for the race. Although displaying the required number 5 on the tail, he decided to incorporate his own quirk to the livery. On the nose the aircraft also displayed the number 57 after his favourite Heinz varieties. A photo appears on the following web page

https://www.uivermemorial.org.au/race.html

The Crew, Aircraft & Achievement

Delving into all the elements of the Race, it was an amazing "can do" mentality and a really enterprising attitude throughout. Yes there were some failures along the way and there were 2 fatalities among the crew. Many however did make the finish.

The excitement amongst spectators all along the route was immense as was the willingness to help when problems occurred.

It cannot be underestimated how momentous this event was for aviation and Mildenhall. The memories show how it drew people from far and wide to a sleepy little town with a half constructed RAF airfield. They were all there from royalty and dignitaries to thousands of spectators eager to enjoy the atmosphere. The weather didn't play ball though. Conditions were noted as being cold, damp and a wind gusting 30mph for the launches starting at 6:30AM.

Further mention must be made of the Comet G-ACSS Grosvenor House. After considerable time and heartache this machine was rebuilt under the umbrella of The Shuttlewoth Collection and even today it can occasionally still be seen flying. Work was carried out at Old Warden, Hatfield and RAE Farnborough. The aircraft is based at Old Warden.

Very few other aircraft have survived in a flying state but 90 years on it's still an eye catching sight.

Finally, Mildenhall recreated spectator enthusiasm during the era of the Mildenhall Air Fetes under the stewardship of the American forces. The period was between 1976 and 2001 and became an international magnet as a major air display in Europe. It is still remembered with great affection for the air shows and amenities though the traffic was also memorable for the wrong reasons. But that's another story and similar to memories of 1934.

Models of the 3 DH.88 Comets

C. W. A. Scott and Tom Campbell Black - 31 - Grosvenor House - G-ACSS - Winner - The Aircraft has been restored and can be seen at The Shuttleworth Collection.

O. Cathcart Jones and K.F. Waller - 19 - G-ACSR - 3rd in the speed race.

Jim Mollison and Amy Johnson - 63 - Black Magic - G-ACSP withdrawn at Jubulpur due to fuel mix up.

64

Suggested further Reading

Podcast from Sept 2019 entitled :-
"The greatest air race: twenty planes, London to Melbourne, 1934"
https://www.abc.net.au/listen/programs/conversations/di-websdale-morrissey-great-air-race/11466948

Air History.net
https://www.airhistory.net/text/2019-09/macrobertson-melbourne-air-race-1934.php

Douglas DC-2 Uiver
https://www.uivermemorial.org.au/race.html

DH88 :-
The Story of de Havilland's Racing Comets - David Ogilvy - Airlife 1984

Scott's Book - C.W.A. Scott (reprint Dec 1934) - Hodder & Stoughton